Bariatric Air Fryer Cookbook

Effortless & Delicious Recipes for Healthier Fried Favorites That Will Help You Eat Well & Keep the Weight Off

Kourla Boran

© Copyright 2020 Kourla Boran - All Rights Reserved.

In no way is it legal to reproduce, duplicate, or transmit any part of this document by either electronic means or in printed format. Recording of this publication is strictly prohibited, and any storage of this material is not allowed unless with written permission from the publisher. All rights reserved.

The information provided herein is stated to be truthful and consistent, in that any liability, regarding inattention or otherwise, by any usage or abuse of any policies, processes, or directions contained within is the solitary and complete responsibility of the recipient reader. Under no circumstances will any legal liability or blame be held against the publisher for any reparation, damages, or monetary loss due to the information herein, either directly or indirectly.

Respective authors own all copyrights not held by the publisher.

Legal Notice:

This book is copyright protected. This is only for personal use. You cannot amend, distribute, sell, use, quote or paraphrase any part of the content within this book without the consent of the author or copyright owner. Legal action will be pursued if this is breached.

Disclaimer Notice:

Please note the information contained within this document is for educational and entertainment purposes only. Every attempt has been made to provide accurate, up-to-date and reliable, complete information. No warranties of any kind are expressed or implied. Readers acknowledge that the author is not engaging in the rendering of legal, financial, medical or professional advice.

By reading this document, the reader agrees that under no circumstances are we responsible for any losses, direct or indirect, which are incurred as a result of the use of information contained within this document, including, but not limited to, errors, omissions, or inaccuracies.

Table of Contents

Introduction 7
Chapter 1: Overview of Bariatric Diet 8
    What is Bariatric Diet? 8
    How to Follow the Bariatric Diet 8
    Foods to Eat & Avoid 8
    Tips on Getting Started 9
Chapter 2: Overview of Air Fryer 10
    What is the Air Fryer? 10
    How Does it Work? 10
    Benefits of Air Frying 10
    Cooking Tips & Tricks 11
Chapter 3: Breakfast Recipes 13
    Baked Eggs 13
    Ham & Egg Toast in Cups 14
    Breakfast Turkey Sausages 15
    Breakfast Burrito 16
    Grilled Cheese Sandwich 17
    Breakfast Potatoes 18
    Hash Brown 19
    French Toast Cups with Blueberries 20
    Breakfast Croquettes 21
    Breakfast Egg Rolls 23
Chapter 4: Fish & Seafood 25
    Coconut Shrimp 25
    Crab Cakes 26
    Salmon & Salad 27

Salmon Cakes 28
Baked Tuna 30
Lemon Herbed Tilapia 31
Cheesy Crabmeat 32
Fish with Garlic & Lemon Pepper 33
Shrimp with Lime & Cumin 34
Cod Fillet with Mustard Sauce 35

Chapter 5: Meat Recipes 37
Steak Salad 37
Sesame Beef Stir Fry 39
Steaks with Chipotle Butter Sauce 41
Cranberry Meatballs 43
Steak with Pepper & Thyme 44
Honey Garlic Pork Chops 45
Ham with Apricot Sauce 46
Sausage, Onion & Bell Peppers 47
Teriyaki Pork 48
Garlic & Rosemary Lamb Chops 49

Chapter 6: Chicken & Poultry Recipes 50
Cajun Chicken 50
Chicken Paprika 52
Korean Fried Chicken 53
Sweet & Sour Chicken 54
Chicken Tikka Masala 55
Herbed Turkey Breast 56
Roasted Maple Turkey 57
Caribbean Chicken 58

Chicken Piccata 59

Thai Chicken 61

Chapter 7: Vegetable Recipes 62

Eggplant Parmesan Casserole 62

Bruschetta 64

Green Beans 65

Corn Fritters 66

Radish Chips 67

Roasted Onion & Cherry Tomatoes 68

Garlic Roasted Carrots 69

Roasted Asparagus & Potatoes 70

Roasted Tomatoes 71

Bok Choy Stir Fry 72

Chapter 8: Snack Recipes 73

Garlic Bread 73

Mozzarella Bites 74

Ranch Pretzels 75

Maple Barbecue Cashews 76

Pizza Bread 77

Mexican Corn 78

Smoky Chickpeas 79

Potato Chips 80

Roasted Macadamia 81

Apricot Brie Snack 82

Chapter 9: Appetizer Recipes 83

Crispy Spinach 83

Buffalo Cauliflower 84

    Stuffed Peppers 85

    Crispy Tofu 87

    Zucchini Fries 88

    Sweet Potato Fries 89

    Salt & Vinegar Wings 90

    Veggie Tots 91

    Tortilla Chips with Salsa 92

    Roasted Olives 94

Chapter 10: Dessert Recipes 95

    Apple Chips 95

    Grilled Pineapple 96

    Watermelon with Mint & Lime 97

    Stuffed Apples 98

    Choco Chip Cookies 99

Chapter 11: 30-Day Meal Plan 100

Conclusion 107

Introduction

Maintaining a healthy weight improves the quality of life and enables us to perform our daily activities with ease and comfort.

Losing a significant amount of excess weight also lowers the risk of obesity-related health conditions, including high cholesterol and blood pressure, type 2 diabetes, and obstructive sleep apnea.

Undergoing bariatric surgery is one way to address obesity. There are several types of bariatric surgery options, including gastric sleeve surgery, gastric bypass surgery, and gastric banding.

Regardless of type, the procedure involves the removal or reduction of the size of your stomach. Bariatric surgery results in rapid weight loss in two ways. You will feel full and stop eating sooner due to your significantly smaller stomach. This translates into the fewer intake of calories. Moreover, there will be a major drop in the levels of the hunger hormone "ghrelin" in your stomach so you will not be as hungry compared to your pre-surgery state.

Within a period of 18 to 24 months, most people who had bariatric surgery can expect to shed off at least 50 percent of their excess body weight. Some people would even lose up to 60 or 70 percent. This is highly possible by staying committed to the recommended diet and exercise plan from your surgery team.

The air fryer is a healthier cooking option that you can explore in making surgery-safe meals. This handy kitchen gadget will help you keep a healthy diet without unnecessary stress and complications.

This cookbook contains easy-to-follow recipes that are both tasty and effective in keeping a healthy weight after bariatric surgery.

Chapter 1: Overview of Bariatric Diet

What is Bariatric Diet?

After bariatric surgery, a surgery team—normally composed of your surgeon and a registered dietician—will explain to you the types and quantity of foods that you can eat. Diet recommendations may vary depending on individual needs.

A bariatric diet is designed to facilitate the healing of your stomach and at the same time, change your eating habits. Sticking to the prescribed diet plan will help you lose weight without side effects and complications.

How to Follow the Bariatric Diet

A bariatric diet is typically structured in stages or phases to help your body to slowly ease back from eating liquids to solids. Most people can consume regular foods again within three months after surgery, depending on how fast the body heals and adjusts to the new eating habits.

Foods to Eat & Avoid

Shortly after the surgery, you will be prescribed a clear liquid only diet. Once your body can handle clear liquids, you can move on to other liquids like broth, milk, unsweetened juice, and decaffeinated coffee or tea.

In the next stage, usually, after your body has tolerated liquids for about a week, you will be allowed to eat 4 to 6 tablespoons of pureed foods per meal. You can have three to six small meals a day.

Within another week, you may be able to add one-third to one-half cup of soft foods to your diet. You can have up to five meals a day and include easy-to-chew foods such as rice, egg, fruits, and cooked vegetables.

After eight weeks, you may slowly start eating firmer foods again and have the usual three meals a day routine. The variety, amount, and consistency of food you can consume will depend on what food and how much your body can tolerate. A daily balanced diet with calories not exceeding 1,000 is recommended.

Avoid foods that may cause pain, nausea, or vomiting such as fried foods, carbonated drinks, bread, raw vegetables, red meat, spicy foods, nuts, and seeds.

Also steer away from fatty and sugary foods to avoid dumping syndrome, as these foods quickly travel through your digestive system.

Tips on Getting Started

Start slow and low. Introduce one new food into your diet at a time, and in small amounts. Also, chew your food slowly.

Keeping hydrated should be a priority. Next, once you passed the clear liquid stage, also focus on eating lean foods that are high in protein.

Always consult with your surgery team before moving on to the next phase of your bariatric diet.

Don't forget to take your prescribed multivitamin supplements. Your body will not be able to absorb enough nutrients from food after the surgery and maybe for the rest of your life.

Chapter 2: Overview of Air Fryer

What is the Air Fryer?

The air fryer is a multifunction kitchen appliance that can give the same crispy results of deep-frying just by using hot air and a tiny amount of oil. It is quite an affordable tool, considering it can also grill, bake, and roast.

How Does it Work?

The air fryer is just like a countertop convection oven, only better and faster. This kitchen gadget features a heating element and a fan that facilitate the rapid circulation of hot air, cooking the food to crispy perfection.

Instead of deep-frying foods, the air fryer uses hot air to induce the Maillard reaction or the phenomenon that gives food its browning color and distinct taste and smell.

Best of all, the air fryer comes with dishwasher-safe parts and accessories, so you get deep fried-like goodness without the usual greasiness and mess.

Benefits of Air Frying

The air fryer is designed to cook a healthier version of deep-fried foods since the latter often contain more fat than those cooked using other methods.

To illustrate, frozen French fries cooked in the air fryer has 4 to 6 grams of fat per serving. The deep-fried version contains 17 grams. A hundred grams of air-fried chicken breast will have 0.39 grams of fat; while the battered deep-fried counterpart contains 13.2 grams of fat.

Requiring just a fraction or to no oil, the air fryer can help cut down the number of calories from fat in your diet. This is beneficial to your health because a high intake of fat may lead to various health conditions, including cardiovascular diseases and inflammations.

Cooking Tips & Tricks

Give your air fryer enough time to pre-heat. Just set the timer for 2 or 3 minutes after turning the air fryer on and setting your desired temperature.

You may be tempted to cook one large batch of food at a time, but don't. Overcrowding the basket of the air fryer often leads to unevenly cook foods. It will also prevent food from crisping and browning. The food may take a longer time to cook, too.

Master the correct way of breading, step by step. We can't stress this enough: breading plays a vital role in many air fryer recipes. The fan of the air fryer can sometimes blow off the breading on the food. You must coat foods in three steps: flour, egg, and then breadcrumbs. Take an especially sweet time with the breadcrumbs, pressing them firmly onto the food.

The fan of the air fryer can also blow light and tiny food particles around, so it is best to secure foods with toothpicks.

Instead of drizzling or brushing oil on the food, use a spray bottle instead. It is not only easier but spraying oil also lets you keep the oil on the food to a minimum. Oil sprays in cans may have aerosol agents in them that can damage the non-stick surface of the air fryer basket so it will be worth it to invest in a hand-pumped kitchen spray bottle.

For an extra browning and crisping of food, spray it with oil halfway through the cooking time. The same timing for flipping foods will also yield more evenly cooked results.

To distribute the ingredients and flavor of the food, you may shake the basket from time to time all throughout the cooking process. This will also create more evenly browned and crisped dishes.

Add water to the air fryer drawer underneath the basket to avoid unnecessary smoking from the grease getting too hot while cooking.

You can open the air fryer as needed to check how the food is coming along. Rest assured that doing so will in no way interrupt the overall cooking process.

Chapter 3: Breakfast Recipes

Baked Eggs

Preparation Time: 10 minutes
Cooking Time: 10 minutes
Serving: 1

Ingredients:

- Cooking spray
- 1 egg
- 1 tablespoon milk
- 2 teaspoons cheese, grated
- 1 tablespoon spinach
- Salt and pepper to taste

Method:

1. Spray your muffin cup with oil.
2. Add the egg, milk, cheese and spinach to the muffin cup.
3. Season with the salt and pepper.
4. Stir the ingredients gently but do not break the egg yolk.
5. Place in the air fryer.
6. Cook at 330 degrees F for 10 minutes.

Serving Suggestions: Garnish with chopped fresh herbs.

Preparation & Cooking Tips: Double or triple the portions but make sure not to overcrowd your air fryer.

Ham & Egg Toast in Cups

Preparation Time: 15 minutes
Cooking Time: 15 minutes
Servings: 4

Ingredients:

- Cooking spray
- 8 whole wheat bread slices
- 2 turkey ham slices, sliced into strips
- 4 eggs
- Salt and pepper to taste

Method:

1. Spray your muffin pan with oil.
2. Flatten the bread slices using a rolling pin.
3. Add the flatten bread slices in the muffin cups.
4. Press it to fit the cups.
5. Add another bread slice on top of the first one.
6. Place the ham strips on top of the bread.
7. Crack an egg into each of the muffin cup.
8. Season with salt and pepper.
9. Add the muffin pan to your air fryer.
10. Cook at 160 degrees F for 15 minutes.

Serving Suggestions: Sprinkle chopped green chives on top.

Preparation & Cooking Tips: You can also add grated cheese on top of the egg.

Breakfast Turkey Sausages

Preparation Time: 5 minutes
Cooking Time: 20 minutes
Servings: 4

Ingredients:

- 4 turkey sausage links

Method:

1. Add the sausages to the air fryer basket.
2. Air fry at 360 degrees F for 15 minutes.
3. Turn the sausages and cook for another 5 minutes.

Serving Suggestions: Serve with fresh green salad.

Preparation & Cooking Tips: Line your air fryer basket with parchment paper to soak up the grease from the sausage.

Breakfast Burrito

Preparation Time: 15 minutes

Cooking Time: 5 minutes

Servings: 6

Ingredients:

- ½ bell pepper, minced
- 6 eggs, scrambled
- ¼ cup turkey bacon, cooked crisp and chopped
- ½ lb. ground sausage, cooked
- ¼ cup cheese, shredded
- 6 tortillas
- Cooking spray

Method:

1. Combine the bell pepper, eggs, bacon, sausage and cheese in a bowl
2. Add the mixture on top of the tortillas.
3. Fold and roll.
4. Add the burritos to the air fryer basket.
5. Spray with oil.
6. Air fry at 330 degrees F for 5 minutes.

Serving Suggestions: Serve with sour cream.

Preparation & Cooking Tips: Make these ahead of time and freeze. Air fry when ready to serve.

Grilled Cheese Sandwich

Preparation Time: 5 minutes

Cooking Time: 7 minutes

Servings: 2

Ingredients:

- 4 slices whole wheat bread
- 1 tablespoon butter, melted
- 2 slices cheddar cheese
- 2 slices mozzarella cheese

Method:

1. Spread the butter on the bread slices.
2. Add the cheese on top of the bread.
3. Top with the other bread slices.
4. Place in the air fryer basket.
5. Air fry at 370 degrees F for 4 minutes.
6. Flip and cook for another 3 minutes.

Serving Suggestions: Serve with fresh green salad.

Preparation & Cooking Tips: You may add ham or turkey bacon to your sandwich.

Breakfast Potatoes

Preparation Time: 10 minutes

Cooking Time: 10 minutes

Servings: 4

Ingredients:

- 1 onion, chopped
- 1 red bell pepper, chopped
- 2 potatoes, sliced into cubes
- Cooking spray
- Salt to taste

Method:

1. Toss the onion, red bell pepper and potatoes in the air fryer basket.
2. Spray with oil.
3. Season with salt.
4. Cook at 400 degrees F for 10 minutes.

Serving Suggestions: Garnish with chopped parsley.

Preparation & Cooking Tips: Check the potatoes during cooking so that they don't get too browned.

Hash Brown

Preparation Time: 30 minutes

Cooking Time: 20 minutes

Servings: 4

Ingredients:

- 1 teaspoon vegetable oil
- 4 potatoes, grated
- 1 teaspoon onion powder
- Salt and pepper to taste
- 2 tablespoons flour

Method:

1. Add the vegetable oil to a pan over medium heat.
2. Cook the grated potatoes for 3 minutes, stirring.
3. Transfer to a plate and let cool.
4. Stir in the remaining ingredients.
5. Form patties from the mixture.
6. Refrigerate for 20 minutes.
7. Place in the air fryer.
8. Air fry at 360 degrees F for 10 minutes per side.

Serving Suggestions: Serve with ketchup.

Preparation & Cooking Tips: Soak the grated potatoes in water to remove starch.

French Toast Cups with Blueberries

Preparation Time: 1 hour and 15 minutes
Cooking Time: 15 minutes
Servings: 4

Ingredients:

- 2 slices whole wheat bread, sliced into cubes
- ½ cup strawberries, sliced
- 2 oz. cream cheese
- 2 eggs, beaten
- ½ cup milk

Method:

1. Add the bread cubes to custard cups or ramekins.
2. Top with the strawberries and cream cheese.
3. Mix the eggs and milk in a bowl.
4. Pour into the custard cups
5. Pour this mixture into the read.
6. Refrigerate for 1 hour.
7. Air fry at 325 degrees F for 15 minutes.

Serving Suggestions: Drizzle with maple syrup.

Preparation & Cooking Tips: Use day-old bread.

Breakfast Croquettes

Preparation Time: 2 hours and 20 minutes

Cooking Time: 17 minutes

Servings: 6

Ingredients:

- 3 tablespoons butter
- 3 tablespoons all-purpose flour
- 3/4 cup nonfat milk
- 6 hard boiled eggs, chopped
- ¼ cup cheddar cheese, shredded
- ½ cup green onions, chopped
- ½ cup fresh asparagus, chopped
- 3 eggs, beaten
- ¾ cup breadcrumbs
- Salt and pepper to taste
- Cooking spray

Method:

1. Add the butter to a pan over medium heat.
2. Melt for 30 seconds.
3. Add the flour and stir.
4. Cook for 1 minute.
5. Stir in the milk, hard boiled eggs, cheese, green onion and asparagus.
6. Transfer the mixture to a bowl.
7. Refrigerate for 2 hours.
8. Form balls from the mixture.

9. Dip in egg.
10. Season with salt and pepper.
11. Dredge with breadcrumbs.
12. Spray with oil.
13. Air fry at 350 degrees F for 10 minutes.
14. Turn and cook for another 5 minutes.

Serving Suggestions: Serve with ketchup.

Preparation & Cooking Tips: You can also add dried tarragon to the mixture.

Breakfast Egg Rolls

Preparation Time: 30 minutes

Cooking Time: 10 minutes

Servings: 12

Ingredients:

- ½ lb. pork sausage, crumbled
- 1 tablespoon green onions, chopped
- 4 eggs, beaten
- 1 tablespoon milk
- Salt and pepper to taste
- ½ cup cheddar cheese, shredded
- ½ cup Monterey Jack cheese, shredded
- 1 tablespoon butter
- 12 egg roll wrappers

Method:

1. Add the pork sausage to a pan over medium heat.
2. Cook for 5 minutes, stirring.
3. Drain the fat.
4. Stir in the green onions.
5. In a bowl, mix the eggs, milk, salt and pepper.
6. Pour mixture into the pan.
7. Cook while stirring for 5 minutes.
8. Add the cheeses.
9. Place mixture on top of the egg wrappers.
10. Roll and seal the edges.

11. Air fry at 400 degrees F for 5 minutes.
12. Turn and cook for another 3 minutes.

Serving Suggestions: Serve with salsa.

Preparation & Cooking Tips: You can also use ground pork or beef for this recipe. Use lean meat.

Chapter 4: Fish & Seafood

Coconut Shrimp

Preparation Time: 15 minutes
Cooking Time: 15 minutes
Servings: 4

Ingredients:

- Salt to taste
- ¼ cup cornstarch
- 2 egg whites
- 1 cup coconut flakes
- ½ lb. shrimp, peeled and deveined
- Cooking spray

Method:

1. Mix the salt and cornstarch in a bowl.
2. In another bowl, beat the egg whites.
3. Place the coconut flakes in the third bowl.
4. Coat the shrimp with cornstarch.
5. Dip in egg and dredge with coconut flakes.
6. Spray shrimp with oil.
7. Place in the air fryer basket.
8. Cook at 330 degrees F for 15 minutes.

Serving Suggestions: Serve with sweet chili sauce.

Preparation & Cooking Tips: You can use frozen peeled shrimp for this recipe.

Crab Cakes

Preparation Time: 15 minutes
Cooking Time: 10 minutes
Servings: 4

Ingredients:

- 8 oz. crab meat
- 1 green onion, chopped
- 2 tablespoons parsley, chopped
- ¼ cup almond flour
- ½ teaspoon Old Bay seasoning
- 1 egg, beaten
- 2 teaspoons Dijon mustard
- Salt and pepper to taste
- Cooking spray

Method:

1. Mix all the ingredients in a bowl.
2. Form patties from the mixture.
3. Spray with oil.
4. Add to the air fryer basket.
5. Cook at 350 degrees F for 5 minutes per side.

Serving Suggestions: Serve with mayo dip.

Preparation & Cooking Tips: Refrigerate crabmeat first for 30 minutes before cooking.

Salmon & Salad

Preparation Time: 10 minutes

Cooking Time: 12 minutes

Servings: 2

Ingredients:

- 2 salmon fillets
- Salt and pepper to taste
- 2 cups lettuce, chopped
- ¼ cup cucumber, chopped
- ¼ cup tomato, chopped
- Vinaigrette

Method:

1. Preheat your air fryer to 350 degrees F.
2. Sprinkle both sides of salmon with the salt and pepper.
3. Add the fish to the air fryer basket.
4. Air fry the salmon for 12 minutes.
5. Toss the lettuce, cucumber and tomato in vinaigrette.
6. Serve salmon with salad.

Serving Suggestions: Garnish with lemon wedges.

Preparation & Cooking Tips: You can also sprinkle fish with fresh herbs before cooking.

Salmon Cakes

Preparation Time: 15 minutes
Cooking Time: 15 minutes
Servings: 4

Ingredients:

Patty

- 1 lb. salmon steaks, diced
- ¼ cup avocado, mashed
- ½ teaspoon curry powder
- ¼ cup cilantro, chopped

Cooking

- ¼ cup tapioca starch
- 2 eggs, beaten
- ½ cup coconut flakes
- Salt to taste

Method:

1. Mix the patty ingredients in a bowl.
2. Form patties from the mixture.
3. Preheat your air fryer to 400 degrees F.
4. Coat the patties with flour.
5. Dip in egg and cover with coconut flakes.
6. Season with the salt.
7. Air fry for 15 minutes, turning once.

Serving Suggestions: Garnish with fresh cilantro.

Preparation & Cooking Tips: Freeze the patties for 30 minutes before dipping in egg and flour.

Baked Tuna

Preparation Time: 5 minutes
Cooking Time: 10 minutes
Servings: 2

Ingredients:

- 2 tuna fillets
- Cooking spray
- Salt and pepper to taste
- 1 teaspoon dried basil

Method:

1. Spray your tuna fillets with oil.
2. Season with salt, pepper and basil.
3. Air fry at 360 degrees F for 5 minutes per side.

Serving Suggestions: Garnish with fresh basil leaves.

Preparation & Cooking Tips: You can also use white fish fillets for this recipe.

Lemon Herbed Tilapia

Preparation Time: 5 minutes

Cooking Time: 8 minutes

Servings: 4

Ingredients:

- 4 tilapia fillets
- Cooking spray
- 1 teaspoon lemon juice
- 1 teaspoon dried oregano
- Salt to taste
- 1 teaspoon garlic powder

Method:

1. Spray the tilapia fillet with oil.
2. In a bowl, mix lemon juice oregano, salt and garlic powder.
3. Spread spice mixture on both sides of fish.
4. Air fry at 400 degrees F for 4 minutes per side.

Serving Suggestions: Garnish with chopped parsley and lemon wedges.

Preparation & Cooking Tips: You can also use cod or haddock for this recipe.

Cheesy Crabmeat

Preparation Time: 1 hour and 20 minutes
Cooking Time: 16 minutes
Servings: 4

Ingredients:

- 6 oz. crab meat
- 2 tablespoons onions, chopped
- ¼ cup celery, chopped
- ¼ cup mayonnaise
- Salt and pepper to taste
- 1/4 cheddar cheese, shredded

Method:

1. Combine the crabmeat, onion, celery, mayo, salt and pepper.
2. Form patties from the mixture.
3. Refrigerate patties for 1 hour.
4. Add the patties to the air fryer basket.
5. Cook at 300 degrees F for 5 to 7 minutes per side.
6. Sprinkle the shredded cheese on top.
7. Cook for another 2 minutes.

Serving Suggestions: Garnish with chopped parsley.

Fish with Garlic & Lemon Pepper

Preparation Time: 10 minutes

Cooking Time: 10 minutes

Servings: 2

Ingredients:

- 2 tilapia fillets
- Cooking spray
- ½ teaspoon garlic powder
- ½ teaspoon onion powder
- ½ teaspoon lemon pepper
- Salt to taste
- Lemon wedges

Method:

1. Preheat your air fryer to 360 degrees F.
2. Spray fish with oil.
3. Sprinkle with garlic powder, onion powder, lemon pepper and salt.
4. Add to the air fryer basket.
5. Top with lemon wedges.
6. Cook at 360 degrees F for 10 minutes.

Serving Suggestions: Garnish with chopped parsley and lemon slices.

Preparation & Cooking Tips: You can also use cod fillets for this recipe.

Shrimp with Lime & Cumin

Preparation Time: 40 minutes

Cooking Time: 10 minutes

Servings: 4

Ingredients:

- 1 lb. shrimp, peeled and deveined

Marinade

- 4 tablespoons lime juice
- 2 teaspoons chipotle in adobo
- 2 tablespoons olive oil
- ¼ teaspoon ground cumin

Method:

1. Combine the marinade ingredients in a bowl.
2. Stir in shrimp.
3. Cover and refrigerate for 30 minutes.
4. Air fry shrimp at 350 degrees F for 10 minutes, turning once.

Serving Suggestions: Garnish with chopped green onion.

Preparation & Cooking Tips: Extend cooking time to 15 minutes if you'll be using frozen shrimp.

Cod Fillet with Mustard Sauce

Preparation Time: 15 minutes
Cooking Time: 15 minutes
Servings: 2

Ingredients:

- Cooking spray
- 2 cod fillets
- 2 tablespoons olive oil
- 1 tablespoon lemon juice
- Salt and pepper to taste

Mustard sauce

- ½ cup heavy cream
- 1 tablespoon butter
- 3 tablespoons mustard
- 1 teaspoon salt

Method:

1. Spray the air fryer basket with oil.
2. Drizzle the cod fillet with olive oil and lemon juice.
3. Season with salt and pepper.
4. Air fry at 350 degrees F for 5 minutes.
5. Increase temperature to 400 degrees F.
6. Cook for another 5 minutes.
7. In a pan over medium heat, add the mustard sauce ingredients.
8. Cook for 3 minutes.

9. Drizzle fish with sauce and serve.

Serving Suggestions: Garnish with lemon slices.

Preparation & Cooking Tips: You can also use tilapia for this recipe.

Chapter 5: Meat Recipes

Steak Salad

Preparation Time: 10 minutes
Cooking Time: 16 minutes
Servings: 4

Ingredients:

- 2 rib eye steaks, fat trimmed and sliced into strips

Marinade

- ¼ cup honey
- 2 teaspoons garlic, minced
- ¼ cup soy sauce
- ¼ cup brown sugar
- ¼ cup Worcestershire sauce

Salad

- 4 cups Romaine lettuce
- 1 cup cherry tomatoes, sliced in half
- ½ cucumber, chopped
- ¼ cup red onions, sliced into rings
- Low-calorie salad dressing

Method:

1. Mix the marinade ingredients in a bowl.
2. Stir in the steak strips.

3. Cover and marinate for 1 hour.
4. Air fry steaks at 400 degrees F for 5 to 8 minutes per side.
5. Let cool.
6. In a bowl, toss the lettuce, tomatoes, cucumber and onions.
7. Top with the steak strips.
8. Drizzle with the dressing.

Serving Suggestions: Serve with main course.

Preparation & Cooking Tips: Use reduced-sodium soy sauce.

Sesame Beef Stir Fry

Preparation Time: 10 minutes

Cooking Time: 10 minutes

Servings: 2

Ingredients:

Marinade

- ¼ cup hoisin sauce
- 2 teaspoons garlic, minced
- 1 tablespoon soy sauce
- 1 teaspoon sesame oil
- 1 teaspoon ground ginger
- ¼ cup water

Stir fry

- 1 lb. flank steak, sliced into strips
- ½ cup broccoli florets
- ½ cup snow peas
- ½ cup carrots, shredded
- ½ cup red onion, sliced

Method:

1. Mix the marinade ingredients in a bowl.
2. Stir in the steak strips.
3. Preheat your air fryer to 400 degrees F for 5 minutes.
4. Add the steak strips and remaining stir fry ingredients.
5. Cook for 10 minutes, stirring every 3 minutes.

Serving Suggestions: Garnish with sesame seeds.

Preparation & Cooking Tips: You can also use carrot strips for this recipe.

Steaks with Chipotle Butter Sauce

Preparation Time: 10 minutes

Cooking Time: 12 minutes

Servings: 2

Ingredients:

Sauce

- ¼ cup butter
- 1 tablespoon chipotle chili
- 1 teaspoon brown sugar
- Salt to taste

Dry rub

- 1 ½ teaspoons chili powder
- 1 teaspoon cocoa powder
- Salt and pepper to taste
- ½ teaspoon brown sugar

Method:

1. Combine dry rub ingredients.
2. Sprinkle both sides of steaks with dry rub mixture.
3. Add steaks to the air fryer basket.
4. Cook at 400 degrees F for 7 minutes.
5. Turn and cook for another 5 minutes.
6. Combine the sauce ingredients.
7. Top the steak with the sauce and serve.

Serving Suggestions: Serve with mashed potatoes.

Preparation & Cooking Tips: Let steaks rest for 10 minutes at room temperature before seasoning.

Cranberry Meatballs

Preparation Time: 5 minutes
Cooking Time: 10 minutes
Servings: 6

Ingredients:

- 28 oz. frozen meatballs
- 14 oz. cranberry jelly sauce
- 12 oz. chili sauce

Method:

1. Add the meatballs to the air fryer basket.
2. Cook at 350 degrees F for 15 minutes, turning once or twice.
3. Heat the jelly sauce and chili sauce in a pan over medium heat.
4. Glaze the meatballs with the mixture and serve.

Serving Suggestions: Garnish with chopped green onions.

Preparation & Cooking Tips: You can also make your own meatballs using ground beef or pork and herbs.

Steak with Pepper & Thyme

Preparation Time: 10 minutes
Cooking Time: 10 minutes
Servings: 4

Ingredients:

- 2 tablespoons olive oil
- 4 tablespoons soy sauce
- 1 tablespoon lemon zest
- 1 teaspoon thyme, chopped
- Salt and pepper to taste
- 1 lb. flank steak

Method:

1. Mix olive oil, soy sauce, lemon zest, thyme, salt and pepper in a bowl.
2. Rub mixture on both sides of steak.
3. Air fry at 400 degrees F for 4 to 5 minutes per side.

Serving Suggestions: Serve with salad.

Preparation & Cooking Tips: Add 2 more minutes to the cooking time if you want your steak more well done.

Honey Garlic Pork Chops

Preparation Time: 10 minutes

Cooking Time: 10 minutes

Servings: 4

Ingredients:

- 4 pork chops
- Salt and pepper to taste
- 4 tablespoons olive oil
- 4 tablespoons garlic, minced
- 4 tablespoons lemon juice
- 2 tablespoons sweet chili sauce
- ½ cup honey

Method:

1. Sprinkle both sides of pork chops with salt and pepper.
2. Air fry pork chops at 400 degrees F for 7 minutes per side.
3. In a pan over medium heat, add the olive oil.
4. Cook the garlic for 1 minute, stirring.
5. Stir in the rest of the ingredients.
6. Cook for 3 minutes.
7. Pour the sauce over the pork chops and serve.

Serving Suggestions: Garnish with fresh herbs.

Preparation & Cooking Tips: Use bone-in pork chops for this recipe.

Ham with Apricot Sauce

Preparation Time: 5 minutes
Cooking Time: 5 minutes
Servings: 2

Ingredients:

- 1 teaspoon lemon juice
- ¼ cup apricot jam
- ½ teaspoon ground cinnamon
- 1 teaspoon mustard
- 2 slices ham

Method:

1. Combine lemon juice, apricot jam, ground cinnamon and mustard in a bowl.
2. Brush both sides of ham with this mixture.
3. Air fry ham at 350 degrees F for 5 minutes.

Serving Suggestions: Drizzle with a little lemon juice before serving.

Preparation & Cooking Tips: Use thick-cut ham slice for this recipe.

Sausage, Onion & Bell Peppers

Preparation Time: 15 minutes

Cooking Time: 10 minutes

Servings: 4

Ingredients:

- 1 onion, sliced
- 1 red bell pepper, sliced
- 1 green bell pepper, sliced
- 2 tablespoons olive oil
- 1 tablespoon Italian seasoning
- 1 lb. bratwurst

Method:

1. Toss the onion and bell peppers in olive oil.
2. Season with Italian seasoning.
3. Stir in bratwurst.
4. Add mixture to the air fryer.
5. Air fry at 400 degrees F for 10 minutes, stirring once or twice.

Serving Suggestions: Serve with ketchup.

Preparation & Cooking Tips: You can also use Italian sausage.

Teriyaki Pork

Preparation Time: 1 day and 10 minutes

Cooking Time: 10 minutes

Servings: 4

Ingredients:

- 1 tablespoon vegetable oil
- 2 tablespoons soy sauce
- 1 tablespoon brown sugar
- 1 tablespoon rice vinegar
- 1 tablespoon garlic, minced
- Salt and pepper to taste
- 1 teaspoon ginger, grated
- 1 lb. pork tenderloin

Method:

1. Combine all the ingredients in a bowl.
2. Cover and marinate for 24 hours.
3. When ready to cook, air fry the pork at 400 degrees F for 20 minutes.
4. Let cool for 10 minutes before slicing and serving.

Serving Suggestions: Garnish with sesame seeds.

Preparation & Cooking Tips: Use lean pork tenderloin.

Garlic & Rosemary Lamb Chops

Preparation Time: 1 hour and 15 minutes

Cooking Time: 10 minutes

Servings: 4

Ingredients:

- 2 tablespoons olive oil
- 4 teaspoons garlic, minced
- 2 tablespoons lemon juice
- 1 teaspoon lemon zest
- 1 tablespoon fresh rosemary, chopped
- Salt and pepper to taste
- 1 lb. lamb chops

Method:

1. Combine olive oil, garlic, lemon juice, lemon zest, rosemary, salt and pepper in a bowl.
2. Add the chops to the marinade.
3. Coat evenly with the sauce.
4. Marinate for 1 hour.
5. Air fry the pork chops at 400 degrees F for 5 minutes per side.

Serving Suggestions: Garnish with fresh rosemary and crispy garlic slices.

Preparation & Cooking Tips: You can also marinate longer for 4 hours in the refrigerator.

Chapter 6: Chicken & Poultry Recipes

Cajun Chicken

Preparation Time: 10 minutes
Cooking Time: 20 minutes
Servings: 8

Ingredients:

- Cooking spray
- 8 chicken drumsticks
- Olive oil

Cajun seasoning

- 1 teaspoon onion powder
- 1 teaspoon paprika
- ½ teaspoon garlic powder
- ½ teaspoon dried thyme
- ½ teaspoon dried basil
- ½ teaspoon dried oregano
- ½ teaspoon cayenne pepper
- Salt and pepper to taste

Method:

1. Combine the Cajun seasoning ingredients.
2. Spray the air fryer basket with oil.
3. Coat chicken with olive oil.
4. Sprinkle all sides of chicken with Cajun seasoning.

5. Add chicken to the air fryer basket.
6. Cook at 400 degrees F for 10 minutes per side.

Serving Suggestions: Garnish with lettuce and cucumber.

Preparation & Cooking Tips: You can also marinate for 30 minutes before cooking.

Chicken Paprika

Preparation Time: 15 minutes

Cooking Time: 30 minutes

Servings: 4

Ingredients:

- 1 lb. chicken wings
- Olive oil
- Salt and pepper to taste
- 1 teaspoon garlic powder
- 3 teaspoons smoked paprika

Method:

1. Drizzle the chicken wings with olive oil.
2. Season with the salt, pepper, garlic powder and smoked paprika.
3. Air fry at 400 degrees F for 30 minutes, turning once or twice.

Serving Suggestions: Garnish with lemon wedges.

Preparation & Cooking Tips: Make sure there's enough room between the chicken wings.

Korean Fried Chicken

Preparation Time: 10 minutes

Cooking Time: 12 minutes

Servings: 4

Ingredients:

- ½ cup flour
- Salt and pepper to taste
- ½ cup water
- 1 lb. chicken
- 1 tablespoon sugar
- 3 teaspoons chili garlic paste
- 1 tablespoon cider vinegar

Method:

1. Mix the flour, salt, pepper and water.
2. Coat the chicken with the batter.
3. Air fry at 350 degrees F for 5 to 8 minutes.
4. In a bowl, mix the remaining ingredients.
5. Toss the chicken in sauce.
6. Air fry at 370 degrees F for 4 minutes.

Serving Suggestions: Garnish with chopped green onion.

Preparation & Cooking Tips: You can also use chicken thigh for this recipe.

Sweet & Sour Chicken

Preparation Time: 10 minutes
Cooking Time: 10 minutes
Servings: 4

Ingredients:

- 1 lb. chicken breast, skinned and sliced into cubes
- ½ cup cornstarch
- Cooking spray

Sauce

- 2 tablespoons chili garlic paste
- 4 tablespoons mayonnaise
- 2 tablespoons rice vinegar
- 6 tablespoons sweet chili sauce

Method:

1. Coat chicken cubes with cornstarch.
2. Spray with oil.
3. Air fry at 400 degrees F for 5 minutes per side.
4. Mix sauce ingredients.
5. Toss the chicken in sauce and serve.

Serving Suggestions: Sprinkle with roasted peanuts.

Preparation & Cooking Tips: You can also use chicken breast fillet for this recipe.

Chicken Tikka Masala

Preparation Time: 45 minutes

Cooking Time: 10 minutes

Servings: 2

Ingredients:

- 3 chicken breast fillets, diced
- 1 bowl tikka masala sauce

Method:

1. Marinate the chicken in the sauce for 30 minutes.
2. Add the chicken to the air fryer.
3. Air fry at 350 degrees F for 5 minutes per side.

Serving Suggestions: Garnish with chopped green onion.

Preparation & Cooking Tips: Remove chicken skin before cooking.

Herbed Turkey Breast

Preparation Time: 5 minutes

Cooking Time: 8 minutes

Servings: 4

Ingredients:

- 4 tablespoons butter, melted
- 1 teaspoon rosemary, chopped
- 1 teaspoon thyme, chopped
- Salt and pepper to taste
- 4 turkey cutlets

Method:

1. Mix the butter, herbs, salt and pepper.
2. Brush both sides of turkey with herb mixture.
3. Air fry at 350 degrees F for 4 minutes per side.

Serving Suggestions: Garnish with lemon wedges.

Preparation & Cooking Tips: You can also use chicken breast fillet for this recipe.

Roasted Maple Turkey

Preparation Time: 10 minutes
Cooking Time: 50 minutes
Servings: 6

Ingredients:

- 4 turkey breast fillets
- 4 tablespoons maple rub
- 4 tablespoons olive oil

Method:

1. Mix the maple rub and olive oil.
2. Brush both sides of turkey with the sauce.
3. Cook the turkey in the air fryer at 350 degrees F for 20 minutes.
4. Baste both sides and cook for another 30 minutes.

Serving Suggestions: Garnish with lettuce and cucumber.

Preparation & Cooking Tips: Let rest for 10 minutes before slicing.

Caribbean Chicken

Preparation Time: 5 minutes
Cooking Time: 15 minutes
Servings: 2

Ingredients:

- 2 chicken breasts
- 2 tablespoons olive oil
- 2 tablespoons jerk seasoning

Method:

1. Drizzle chicken with oil.
2. Season both sides with jerk seasoning.
3. Air fry at 370 degrees F for 15 minutes, turning once or twice.

Serving Suggestions: Serve with salsa.

Preparation & Cooking Tips: You can also season with salt and pepper in addition to jerk seasoning.

Chicken Piccata

Preparation Time: 15 minutes

Cooking Time: 13 minutes

Servings: 4

Ingredients:

Chicken

- 4 chicken breast fillets
- Salt and pepper to taste
- 1 teaspoon garlic powder
- 1 egg white
- 1 tablespoon lemon juice
- ½ cup Italian bread crumbs

Sauce

- 1 tablespoon butter
- 2 tablespoons lemon juice
- ¾ cup chicken broth
- 1 tablespoon capers
- Salt and pepper to taste

Method:

1. Flatten chicken with meat mallet.
2. In a bowl, mix garlic powder, egg and lemon juice.
3. Season chicken with salt and pepper.
4. Dip in the egg mixture.
5. Dredge with breadcrumbs.

6. Air fry at 350 degrees F for 5 minutes per side.
7. In a pan, cook the sauce ingredients for 3 minutes.
8. Drizzle the chicken with the sauce and serve.

Serving Suggestions: Garnish with lemon wedges.

Preparation & Cooking Tips: Use low-sodium chicken broth.

Thai Chicken

Preparation Time: 10 minutes
Cooking Time: 20 minutes
Servings: 2

Ingredients:

- 2 chicken breast fillets, diced
- 1 cup Thai peanut sauce

Method:

1. Marinate chicken breast fillet with half of the peanut sauce for 1 hour.
2. Air fry at 350 degrees F for 5 to 10 minutes per side

Serving Suggestions: Serve with Jasmine rice

Preparation & Cooking Tips: Baste with peanut sauce before serving.

Chapter 7: Vegetable Recipes

Eggplant Parmesan Casserole

Preparation Time: 15 minutes
Cooking Time: 27 minutes
Servings: 4

Ingredients:

- 1 eggplant, peeled and sliced
- 2 teaspoons salt
- 1 egg, beaten
- ¼ cup milk
- 1 cup breadcrumbs
- 1 cup tomato sauce
- ½ cup mozzarella cheese, shredded
- ¼ cup Parmesan cheese, grated

Method:

1. Arrange the eggplant on a plate.
2. Sprinkle with salt.
3. Let sit for 10 minutes.
4. Beat egg and milk in a bowl.
5. Add breadcrumbs in another bowl.
6. Dip each eggplant slice in the egg mixture.
7. Dredge with breadcrumbs.
8. Air fry at 320 degrees F for 6 minutes per side.
9. Spread tomato sauce on a small baking pan.

10. Top with the eggplant
11. Sprinkle cheese on top.
12. Air fry at 320 degrees F for 15 minutes

Serving Suggestions: Garnish with chopped basil.

Preparation & Cooking Tips: Use Italian breadcrumbs for this recipe.

Bruschetta

Preparation Time: 15 minutes
Cooking Time: 3 minutes
Servings: 12

Ingredients:

- 4 tomatoes, chopped
- 1 tablespoon garlic, minced
- ¼ cup Parmesan cheese, shredded
- ¼ cup fresh basil leaves, chopped
- 1 teaspoon olive oil
- 1 tablespoon vinegar
- Salt and pepper to taste
- 1 loaf French bread, sliced

Method:

1. In a bowl, mix all the ingredients except the bread.
2. Let sit for 10 minutes.
3. Spread the mixture on top of the bread slices.
4. Air fry at 250 degrees F for 3 minutes.

Serving Suggestions: Serve immediately.

Preparation & Cooking Tips: Use balsamic vinegar for this recipe.

Green Beans

Preparation Time: 5 minutes
Cooking Time: 9 minutes
Servings: 4

Ingredients:

- 1 lb. green beans, trimmed
- 4 tablespoons sesame oil
- 4 teaspoons red wine vinegar
- 4 teaspoons soy sauce
- 2 cloves garlic, minced

Method:

1. Toss the green beans in the oil, vinegar, soy sauce and garlic.
2. Add the green beans with sauce to the air fryer.
3. Cook at 400 degrees F for 6 minutes.
4. Stir and cook for another 3 minutes.

Serving Suggestions: Garnish with pepper.

Corn Fritters

Preparation Time: 10 minutes

Cooking Time: 6 minutes

Servings: 4

Ingredients:

- 1 ½ cup corn kernels
- 1 teaspoon sugar
- ½ cup all-purpose flour
- Salt and pepper to taste
- 1 egg, beaten
- ¼ cup milk
- 2 stalks green onion, chopped
- ½ cup cheddar cheese, shredded

Method:

1. Mix the corn, sugar, flour, salt and pepper in a bowl.
2. Stir in the egg and milk.
3. Add the green onion and cheese.
4. Pour 3 tablespoons of the mixture on the air fryer tray.
5. Air fry at 350 degrees F for 3 minutes per side.

Serving Suggestions: Serve with sour cream and chopped chives.

Preparation & Cooking Tips: You can use almond milk for this recipe.

Radish Chips

Preparation Time: 10 minutes
Cooking Time: 10 minutes
Servings: 2

Ingredients:

- 1 lb. radish, sliced into rounds
- 2 tablespoons olive oil
- Salt and pepper to taste

Method:

1. Coat the radish with olive oil.
2. Season with salt and pepper.
3. Place in the air fryer.
4. Cook at 390 degrees F for 10 minutes, stirring once or twice.

Serving Suggestions: Serve with your favorite low-fat dip.

Preparation & Cooking Tips: Dry the radish thoroughly before seasoning.

Roasted Onion & Cherry Tomatoes

Preparation Time: 5 minutes

Cooking Time: 5 minutes

Servings: 4

Ingredients:

- 1 lb. cherry tomatoes
- 2 tablespoons olive oil
- 1 teaspoon Italian seasoning
- Salt and pepper to taste
- 1 onion, roasted and sliced into wedges

Method:

1. Toss the tomatoes in olive oil.
2. Season with Italian herbs, salt and pepper.
3. Add to the air fryer basket.
4. Cook at 300 degrees F for 5 minutes.
5. Stir in the onion and serve.

Serving Suggestions: Drizzle with a little olive oil before serving.

Preparation & Cooking Tips: You can also use other dried herbs for this recipe.

Garlic Roasted Carrots

Preparation Time: 10 minutes

Cooking Time: 10 minutes

Servings: 4

Ingredients:

- 1 lb. carrots, diced
- 2 tablespoons olive oil
- Salt and pepper to taste
- 2 teaspoons garlic powder

Method:

1. Coat the carrots with the olive oil.
2. Season with the salt, pepper and garlic powder.
3. Transfer to the air fryer basket.
4. Cook at 390 degrees F for 10 minutes, stirring once.

Serving Suggestions: Serve with maple syrup.

Preparation & Cooking Tips: Do not overcrowd the air fryer basket.

Roasted Asparagus & Potatoes

Preparation Time: 10 minutes
Cooking Time: 7 minutes
Servings: 4

Ingredients:

- Water
- 1 lb. asparagus, trimmed
- 2 stalks scallions, chopped
- 4 potatoes, roasted
- 1 tablespoon olive oil
- 1 teaspoon dried dill
- Salt and pepper to taste

Method:

1. Fill a pot with water.
2. Add the asparagus.
3. Boil for 2 minutes.
4. Drain.
5. Chop into smaller pieces.
6. Combine the boiled asparagus and the rest of the ingredients in a bowl.
7. Air fry at 350 degrees F for 5 minutes.

Serving Suggestions: Garnish with herb sprigs.

Preparation & Cooking Tips: You can also add other herbs to this recipe.

Roasted Tomatoes

Preparation Time: 5 minutes

Cooking Time: 5 minutes

Servings: 4

Ingredients:

- 1 lb. tomatoes, sliced into quarters
- ½ cup balsamic vinegar
- 1 teaspoon Italian seasoning

Method:

1. Toss the tomatoes in balsamic vinegar.
2. Sprinkle with the Italian seasoning.
3. Spread tomatoes in the air fryer basket.
4. Cook at 300 degrees F for 5 minutes, stirring once.

Serving Suggestions: Sprinkle with dried herbs before serving.

Preparation & Cooking Tips: You can also use cherry tomatoes for this recipe.

Bok Choy Stir Fry

Preparation Time: 10 minutes

Cooking Time: 10 minutes

Servings: 4

Ingredients:

- 1 lb. bok choy, rinsed and drained
- 1 tablespoon oyster sauce
- 3 tablespoons chicken broth
- 2 tablespoons peanut oil
- 2 cloves garlic, minced
- Salt to taste

Method:

1. Mix all the ingredients in a bowl.
2. Add the bok choy to your air fryer.
3. Air fry at 350 degrees F for 10 minutes, stirring twice.

Serving Suggestions: Garnish with crispy garlic slices.

Preparation & Cooking Tips: Use low sodium oyster sauce.

Chapter 8: Snack Recipes

Garlic Bread

Preparation Time: 5 minutes
Cooking Time: 5 minutes
Servings: 2

Ingredients:

- ½ cup butter, melted
- Pinch salt
- 1 tablespoon fresh parsley, chopped
- 4 cloves garlic, roasted and minced
- 1 loaf French bread, sliced in half lengthwise

Method:

1. Mix the butter, salt, parsley and garlic in a bowl.
2. Spread mixture on top of French bread.
3. Air fry at 400 degrees F for 3 minutes.
4. Let cool for 2 minutes before serving.

Serving Suggestions: Serve with pasta dish.

Preparation & Cooking Tips: You can also use dried parsley.

Mozzarella Bites

Preparation Time: 5 minutes
Cooking Time: 5 minutes
Servings: 4

Ingredients:

- 8 mozzarella sticks
- 2 tablespoons butter
- ¼ breadcrumbs

Method:

1. Dip the mozzarella sticks in butter.
2. Dredge with breadcrumbs.
3. Arrange in the air fryer basket.
4. Cook at 320 degrees F for 5 minutes, stirring once.

Serving Suggestions: Serve with marinara dipping sauce.

Preparation & Cooking Tips: Use panko breadcrumbs for this recipe.

Ranch Pretzels

Preparation Time: 5 minutes

Cooking Time: 5 minutes

Servings: 4

Ingredients:

- 10 oz. pretzels
- 2 tablespoons olive oil
- 1 packet dry ranch seasoning mix

Method:

1. Coat the pretzels with olive oil.
2. Sprinkle all sides with ranch seasoning.
3. Arrange the pretzels in the air fryer basket.
4. Cook at 320 degrees F for 3 minutes.
5. Turn and cook for another 2 minutes.

Serving Suggestions: Let cool for 10 minutes before serving.

Preparation & Cooking Tips: Store in an airtight jar for up to 3 days.

Maple Barbecue Cashews

Preparation Time: 5 minutes

Cooking Time: 5 minutes

Servings: 12

Ingredients:

- 2 tablespoons olive oil
- 2 teaspoons maple barbecue rub
- 1 cup raw cashews

Method:

1. Blend olive oil and maple barbecue rub.
2. Coat cashews with this mixture.
3. Add to the air fryer basket.
4. Air fry at 370 degrees F for 5 minutes, stirring once.

Serving Suggestions: Let cool before serving.

Preparation & Cooking Tips: Store in an airtight jar for up to 3 days.

Pizza Bread

Preparation Time: 10 minutes

Cooking Time: 5 minutes

Servings: 4

Ingredients:

- 1 cup marinara sauce
- 2 French bread, sliced in half lengthwise
- ½ cup mozzarella sauce, shredded
- 1 tablespoon fresh parsley, chopped
- 1 tablespoon fresh oregano, chopped

Method:

1. Spread marina sauce on top of bread.
2. Sprinkle the mozzarella cheese on top.
3. Add the chopped herbs on top.
4. Air fry at 400 degrees F for 5 minutes.

Serving Suggestions: Sprinkle with Parmesan cheese before serving.

Preparation & Cooking Tips: Use low-sodium marinara sauce.

Mexican Corn

Preparation Time: 5 minutes

Cooking Time: 10 minutes

Servings: 4

Ingredients:

- 4 ears corn
- ¼ cup Cotija cheese, crumbled
- ¼ cup fresh cilantro, chopped
- ¼ teaspoon chili powder

Method:

1. Add the corn to the air fryer basket.
2. Air fry at 390 degrees F for 10 minutes.
3. Sprinkle with the Cotija cheese.
4. Cook for 5 more minutes.
5. Sprinkle with the cilantro and chili powder.

Serving Suggestions: Garnish with lime wedges.

Preparation & Cooking Tips: You can also use other types of cheese like feta.

Smoky Chickpeas

Preparation Time: 5 minutes
Cooking Time: 18 minutes
Servings: 4

Ingredients:

- 15 oz. chickpeas, rinsed and drained
- 1 tablespoon sunflower oil
- Salt to taste
- 2 tablespoons lemon juice
- ½ teaspoon ground cumin
- ¾ teaspoon smoked paprika
- ½ teaspoon granulated garlic

Method:

1. Preheat your air fryer to 390 degrees F.
2. Cook chickpeas for 15 minutes, shaking the basket once.
3. In a bowl, mix the oil, salt, lemon juice and spices.
4. Toss the chickpeas in the spice mixture.
5. Air fry at 360 degrees F for 3 minutes.

Serving Suggestions: Let cool before serving or storing.

Potato Chips

Preparation Time: 5 minutes
Cooking Time: 15 minutes
Servings: 4

Ingredients:

- Cooking spray
- 1 potato, sliced thinly
- Salt to taste

Method:

1. Spray your air fryer basket with oil.
2. Spray the potato slices with oil.
3. Sprinkle potato with salt.
4. Air fry at 450 degrees F for 15 minutes, stirring once or twice.

Serving Suggestions: Sprinkle with Parmesan cheese before serving.

Preparation & Cooking Tips: Use mandolin to slice potato thinly.

Roasted Macadamia

Preparation Time: 5 minutes
Cooking Time: 10 minutes
Servings: 4

Ingredients:

- 1 lb. macadamia nuts
- Salt to taste

Method:

1. Spread the macadamia nuts in the air fryer basket.
2. Cook at 250 degrees F for 10 minutes, shaking the basket halfway through.
3. Sprinkle with salt.

Serving Suggestions: Sprinkle with herbs or grated Parmesan cheese.

Preparation & Cooking Tips: Store in an airtight container for up to 3 days.

Apricot Brie Snack

Preparation Time: 10 minutes
Cooking Time: 5 minutes
Servings: 8

Ingredients:

- 1 package crescent dough sheets
- 4 oz. brie cheese, sliced
- ½ cup apricot preserves

Method:

1. Spread the crescent dough sheet on your kitchen table.
2. Press the sheet onto muffin cups.
3. Top with the cheese and apricot preserves.
4. Air fry at 340 degrees F for 5 minutes.

Serving Suggestions: Let cool before serving.

Preparation & Cooking Tips: You can also use raspberry preserves for this recipe.

Chapter 9: Appetizer Recipes

Crispy Spinach

Preparation Time: 10 minutes

Cooking Time: 10 minutes

Servings: 4

Ingredients:

- 4 cups baby spinach leaves
- Cooking spray
- 1 tablespoon Parmesan cheese

Method:

1. Spray baby spinach with oil.
2. Air fry at 300 degrees F for 10 minutes.
3. Sprinkle with the Parmesan cheese.

Serving Suggestions: Drizzle with lemon juice before serving.

Preparation & Cooking Tips: You can also use regular spinach but slice into smaller portions.

Buffalo Cauliflower

Preparation Time: 10 minutes
Cooking Time: 15 minutes
Servings: 8

Ingredients:

- Cooking spray
- 8 cups cauliflower florets
- 1 cup buffalo sauce

Method:

1. Preheat your air fryer to 360 degrees F.
2. Spray your air fryer basket with oil.
3. Add the cauliflower florets to the air fryer.
4. Air fry for 15 minutes, flipping every 5 minutes.

Serving Suggestions: Serve with low-fat ranch dressing.

Stuffed Peppers

Preparation Time: 20 minutes
Cooking Time: 30 minutes
Servings: 4

Ingredients:

- 1 teaspoon olive oil
- ½ cup onion, chopped
- ½ lb. ground beef
- ¼ teaspoon garlic powder
- Salt and pepper to taste
- 1 cup tomato sauce
- 1 cup brown rice, cooked
- 3 bell peppers, sliced in half
- ¾ cup mozzarella cheese

Method:

1. Add the olive oil to a pan over medium heat.
2. Cook the onion and ground beef for 5 minutes.
3. Season with garlic powder, salt and pepper.
4. Stir in the tomato sauce and rice.
5. Cook for 5 more minutes.
6. Transfer the beef mixture to a plate.
7. Stuff the peppers halved with the mixture.
8. Place these on the air fryer tray.
9. Air fry at 360 degrees F for 15 minutes.
10. Sprinkle cheese on top and cook for another 5 minutes.

Serving Suggestions: Garnish with dried herbs.

Preparation & Cooking Tips: Use bell peppers of different colors.

Crispy Tofu

Preparation Time: 15 minutes

Cooking Time: 15 minutes

Servings: 4

Ingredients:

- 12 oz. tofu, sliced into cubes
- 1 tablespoon avocado oil
- 1 teaspoon onion powder
- 1 teaspoon garlic powder
- 1 teaspoon paprika
- 2 teaspoons cornstarch
- Salt and pepper to taste

Method:

1. Preheat your air fryer to 390 degrees F.
2. Toss the tofu cubes in oil.
3. Combine the remaining ingredients in a bowl.
4. Coat the tofu cubes with the cornstarch mixture.
5. Air fry at 15 minutes, shaking every 5 minutes.

Serving Suggestions: Serve with choice dipping sauce.

Preparation & Cooking Tips: Press tofu to get rid of extra moisture before closing.

Zucchini Fries

Preparation Time: 15 minutes
Cooking Time: 10 minutes
Servings: 6

Ingredients:

- 2 zucchinis, sliced into strips
- ½ cup flour
- 3 eggs
- Salt and pepper to taste
- 1 cup breadcrumbs
- 1 teaspoon cumin
- 1 tablespoon olive oil
- ¼ cup Parmesan cheese

Method:

1. Coat zucchini strips with flour.
2. In a bowl, beat eggs, salt and pepper.
3. Dip zucchini in egg mixture.
4. In the third bowl, combine remaining ingredients.
5. Coat zucchini with Parmesan cheese mixture.
6. Air fry at 400 degrees F for 10 minutes.

Serving Suggestions: Sprinkle with salt and pepper before serving.

Preparation & Cooking Tips: You can also use carrots for this recipe.

Sweet Potato Fries

Preparation Time: 10 minutes
Cooking Time: 15 minutes
Servings: 2

Ingredients:

- Cooking spray
- 2 sweet potatoes, sliced into strips
- 2 teaspoons olive oil
- ¼ teaspoon sweet paprika
- ½ teaspoon garlic powder
- Salt and pepper to taste

Method:

1. Preheat your air fryer to 400 degrees F.
2. Spray your air fryer basket with oil.
3. Toss sweet potatoes in olive oil.
4. Season with paprika, garlic powder, salt and pepper.
5. Air fry at 15 minutes, stirring once or twice.

Serving Suggestions: Serve with mayo dipping sauce.

Preparation & Cooking Tips: You can also use garlic salt instead of garlic powder and salt.

Salt & Vinegar Wings

Preparation Time: 5 minutes
Cooking Time: 17 minutes
Servings: 8

Ingredients:

- 2 lb. chicken wings

Marinade

- 2 ¼ dry ranch mix
- 6 tablespoons apple cider vinegar
- ½ cup white vinegar
- 1 teaspoon garlic power
- 1 teaspoon sugar
- Salt to taste

Method:

1. Combine the marinade ingredients in a bowl.
2. Stir in the chicken.
3. Cover and marinate for 30 minutes.
4. Add to the air fryer basket.
5. Air fry at 380 degrees F for 6 minutes per side.
6. Increase heat to 400 degrees F.
7. Cook for another 5 minutes.

Serving Suggestions: Garnish with chopped green onions.

Preparation & Cooking Tips: You can also use chicken drumsticks for this recipe.

Veggie Tots

Preparation Time: 5 minutes

Cooking Time: 8 minutes

Servings: 4

Ingredients:

- 1 package frozen veggie tots
- Cooking spray

Method:

1. Spread the veggie tots in the air fryer basket.
2. Spray with oil.
3. Air fry at 400 degrees F for 4 minutes per side.

Serving Suggestions: Serve with low-fat and low-calorie dipping sauce.

Tortilla Chips with Salsa

Preparation Time: 5 minutes
Cooking Time: 8 minutes
Servings: 4

Ingredients:

- 4 corn tortillas
- 4 tablespoons olive oil
- Salt to taste

Salsa

- 28 oz. tomatoes, chopped
- 2 tablespoons onion, minced
- 1 clove garlic, minced
- 1 jalapeno pepper, chopped
- ½ cup cilantro, chopped
- 2 tablespoons lime juice
- 1 teaspoon ground cumin
- Salt to taste

Method:

1. Slice tortillas into wedges.
2. Brush tortilla pieces with oil.
3. Sprinkle with salt.
4. Add to the air fryer.
5. Air fry at 320 degrees F for 4 minutes per side.
6. Mix the salsa ingredients.

7. Serve the tortilla chips with salsa.

Serving Suggestions: Serve with sour cream.

Preparation & Cooking Tips: You can also serve with ready-made salsa.

Roasted Olives

Preparation Time: 5 minutes
Cooking Time: 5 minutes
Servings: 4

Ingredients:

- 1 cup green olives
- 1 cup black olives
- 2 tablespoons olive oil
- 2 teaspoons garlic, minced
- ½ teaspoon dried oregano
- Salt and pepper to taste

Method:

1. Coat the olives with oil.
2. Season with garlic, herbs, salt and pepper.
3. Air fry at 300 degrees F for 5 minutes.

Serving Suggestions: Serve with cheese and cold cuts.

Chapter 10: Dessert Recipes

Apple Chips

Preparation Time: 10 minutes
Cooking Time: 10 minutes
Servings: 4

Ingredients:

- 3 apples, sliced thinly
- 1 tablespoon ground cinnamon
- ¼ cup melted butter

Method:

1. Add apple slices to the air fryer basket.
2. Brush apple slices with butter.
3. Sprinkle both sides with cinnamon.
4. Air fry at 300 degrees F for 7 minutes per side.

Serving Suggestions: Drizzle with a teaspoon of melted butter before serving.

Preparation & Cooking Tips: Use mandolin to slice apples thinly.

Grilled Pineapple

Preparation Time: 5 minutes

Cooking Time: 10 minutes

Servings: 4

Ingredients:

- 1 cup pineapple slices
- 2 tablespoons butter
- 3 tablespoons brown sugar

Method:

1. Brush pineapple slices with butter.
2. Sprinkle both sides with brown sugar.
3. Air fry at 400 degrees F for 3 minutes.

Serving Suggestions: Serve with maple syrup.

Preparation & Cooking Tips: You can use canned pineapple.

Watermelon with Mint & Lime

Preparation Time: 10 minutes
Cooking Time: 10 minutes
Servings: 4

Ingredients:

- 1 watermelon, sliced
- 2 tablespoons lime juice
- 1 tablespoon olive oil
- 2 tablespoons mint leaves
- Salt to taste

Method:

1. Mix lime juice, olive oil, mint leaves and salt in a bowl.
2. Brush both sides of watermelon with this mixture.
3. Air fry watermelon at 400 degrees F for 5 minutes per side.

Serving Suggestions: Garnish with fresh mint leaves.

Stuffed Apples

Preparation Time: 10 minutes
Cooking Time: 20 minutes
Servings: 1

Ingredients:

- 2 tablespoons walnuts
- 1 tablespoon butter
- 2 tablespoons raisins
- Pinch ground nutmeg
- 1 apple, sliced in half

Method:

1. Add walnuts, butter and raisins on top of the apples.
2. Sprinkle with nutmeg.
3. Air fry at 350 degrees F for 20 minutes.

Serving Suggestions: Drizzle with maple syrup.

Choco Chip Cookies

Preparation Time: 10 minutes

Cooking Time: 6 minutes

Servings: 12

Ingredients:

- 1 box yellow cake mix
- 1/3 cup melted butter
- 2 eggs, beaten
- 1 cup chocolate chips

Method:

1. Mix all the ingredients in a bowl.
2. Form cookies from the mixture.
3. Add to the air fryer basket.
4. Cook at 330 degrees F for 6 minutes.

Serving Suggestions: Let cool before serving.

Preparation & Cooking Tips: Store in an airtight container for up to 2 days.

Chapter 11: 30-Day Meal Plan

In the final stage of the bariatric diet, you will be able to slowly return to a resemblance to a regular diet.

At this point, you would have fully adapted and incorporated your new eating habits into your lifestyle.

You are ready to maintain a healthy diet that will not compromise all your efforts in reaching your ideal weight.

Below is a menu plan that features surgery-safe tasty dishes that you can cook with your air fryer for 30 days.

Day 1

Breakfast: Baked Eggs

Lunch: Coconut Shrimp

Dinner: Eggplant Parmesan Casserole

Day 2

Breakfast: Ham & Egg Toast in Cups

Lunch: Crab Cakes

Dinner: Bruschetta

Day 3

Breakfast: Breakfast Turkey Sausages

Lunch: Salmon & Salad

Dinner: Green Beans

Day 4

Breakfast: Breakfast Burrito

Lunch: Salmon Cakes

Dinner: Corn Fritters

Day 5

Breakfast: Grilled Cheese Sandwich

Lunch: Baked Tuna

Dinner: Radish Chips

Day 6

Breakfast: Breakfast Potatoes

Lunch: Lemon Herbed Tilapia

Dinner: Roasted Onion & Cherry Tomatoes

Day 7

Breakfast: Hash Brown

Lunch: Cheesy Crabmeat

Dinner: Garlic Roasted Carrots

Day 8

Breakfast: French Toast Cups with Blueberries

Lunch: Fish With Garlic & Lemon Pepper

Dinner: Roasted Asparagus & Potatoes

Day 9

Breakfast: Breakfast Croquettes

Lunch: Shrimp with Lime & Cumin

Dinner: Roasted Tomatoes

Day 10

Breakfast: Breakfast Egg Rolls

Lunch: Cod Fillet with Mustard Sauce

Dinner: Bok Choy Stir Fry

Day 11

Breakfast: Baked Eggs

Lunch: Steak Salad

Dinner: Steak Salad

Day 12

Breakfast: Ham & Egg Toast in Cups

Lunch: Sesame Beef Stir Fry

Dinner: Chicken Piccata

Day 13

Breakfast: Breakfast Turkey Sausages

Lunch: Steaks with Chipotle Butter Sauce

Dinner: Garlic & Rosemary Lamb Chops

Day 14

Breakfast: Breakfast Burrito

Lunch: Cranberry Meatballs

Dinner: Honey Garlic Pork Chops

Day 15

Breakfast: Grilled Cheese Sandwich

Lunch: Steak with Pepper & Thyme

Dinner: Baked Tuna

Day 16

Breakfast: Breakfast Potatoes

Lunch: Honey Garlic Pork Chops

Dinner: Roasted Maple Turkey

Day 17

Breakfast: Hash Brown

Lunch: Ham with Apricot Sauce

Dinner: Bok Choy Stir Fry

Day 18

Breakfast: French Toast Cups with Blueberries

Lunch: Sausage, Onion & Bell Peppers

Dinner: Caribbean Chicken

Day 19

Breakfast: Breakfast Croquettes

Lunch: Teriyaki Pork

Dinner: Lemon Herbed Tilapia

Day 20

Breakfast: Breakfast Egg Rolls

Lunch: Garlic & Rosemary Lamb Chops

Dinner: Steaks with Chipotle Butter Sauce

Day 21

Breakfast: Baked Eggs

Lunch: Cajun Chicken

Dinner: Fish with Garlic & Lemon Pepper

Day 22

Breakfast: Ham & Egg Toast in Cups

Lunch: Chicken Paprika

Dinner: Sausage, Onion & Bell Peppers

Day 23

Breakfast: Breakfast Turkey Sausages

Lunch: Korean Fried Chicken

Dinner: Eggplant Parmesan Casserole

Day 24

Breakfast: Breakfast Burrito

Lunch: Sweet & Sour Chicken

Dinner: Herbed Turkey Breast

Day 25

Breakfast: Grilled Cheese Sandwich

Lunch: Chicken Tikka Masala

Dinner: Shrimp with Lime & Cumin

Day 26

Breakfast: Breakfast Potatoes

Lunch: Herbed Turkey Breast

Dinner: Cheesy Crabmeat

Day 27

Breakfast: Hash Brown

Lunch: Roasted Maple Turkey

Dinner: Teriyaki Pork

Day 28

Breakfast: French Toast Cups with Blueberries

Lunch: Caribbean Chicken

Dinner: Sausage, Onion & Bell Peppers

Day 29

Breakfast: Breakfast Croquettes

Lunch: Chicken Piccata

Dinner: Sweet & Sour Chicken

Day 30

Breakfast: Breakfast Egg Rolls

Lunch: Thai Chicken

Dinner: Steak with Pepper & Thyme

Conclusion

By reducing the size of your stomach, a bariatric surgery changes the way food enters your intestines. After the procedure, getting adequate nourishment while losing weight is of prime importance.

An air fryer is a slick gadget that supports the low-fat requirement of a bariatric diet. With this kitchen appliance, you will make delicious and nutritious surgery-safe foods with ease and speed.

Transitioning into a healthier lifestyle that supports your weight-loss goals will take effort that with proper meal planning and a versatile tool like the air fryer, nothing is impossible.

Of course, regular follow-up visits with your surgery team will determine your long-term safety and success. After completing the scheduled appointments during the first year, getting checked annually is recommended.

www.ingramcontent.com/pod-product-compliance
Lightning Source LLC
Chambersburg PA
CBHW081403070526
44583CB00020B/2663